NBA ALL-STAR KEVIN GARNETT

by Steve Aschburner

SCHOLASTIC INC.
New York   Toronto   London   Auckland   Sydney
Mexico City   New Delhi   Hong Kong   Buenos Aires

To G. and G.

PHOTO CREDITS
NBA Entertainment Photos
Cover, 4, 25, 30, 33: David Sherman. 5: David Liam Kyle. 7, 20, 21, 27, 28, 31, 34, 35: Andrew D. Bernstein. 22: Barry Gossage. 23: Dale Tait. 29: Andy Hayt. 32: Noren Trotman. 37, 38: Jesse D. Garrabrant. 39: Nathaniel S. Butler. 40: Glenn James.
8, 12, 14, 16: Courtesy of the Garnett family.

ISBN 0-439-34305-4

12 11 10 9 8 7 6 5 4 3 2   2 3 4 5 6/0 1

Printed in the U.S.A.
First Scholastic printing, December 2001
Book design by Carisa Swenson

Contents

Kevin Garnett loves to surprise people. He's only 25 years old, but he is already a superstar. That's a big surprise, because most basketball players his age are only just starting to be great NBA stars. But Kevin joined the NBA when he was only 19 years old. He surprised a lot of people because he came straight to the NBA from high school and was a big success.

Kevin is almost seven feet tall! He is a big player who is great at jumping and rebounding. Many people whom Kevin plays basketball with think that he will be slow because he is so tall and lanky. But Kevin surprises them all by making quick and exciting moves and shots. He loves to play basketball and that's what makes him great.

Even though he is from a small town in South Carolina, Kevin knows a lot of things about the world. He also has a lot of energy on the court. Because he's so exciting to watch, Kevin is popular with his teammates and fans. Kevin is a wizard on defense. He can guard anyone — Tim Duncan, Kobe Bryant, Jason Kidd or Michael Finley.

Kevin was also an important member of the USA Men's Olympic Basketball Team. Kevin and his teammates won a gold medal at the 2000 Olympics in Australia!

He has played in four NBA All-Star Games. Kevin is also the best player who has ever played for the Minnesota Timberwolves. But best of all, he is a great guy. Kevin is a fun player who always cares about others and who loves to win.

Kevin wants to play in the NBA for a long time. But only if he keeps winning. More than anything, Kevin wants to help the Timberwolves win an NBA championship. Other great players won many titles for their team very quickly. Magic Johnson won three NBA titles in his first six years. Kobe Bryant won two titles in his first five years and Tim Duncan won one in his second season. Kevin would like to win one, too.

"I really want the Timberwolves to be successful," Kevin said. "This team has been down so much that anything I can do to help us say 'We're winners,' I'm going to do it. I want to be the best. Period."

Chapter Two

Kevin Maurice Garnett was born on May 19, 1976. He grew up on Basswood Drive in Maudlin, South Carolina. His neighborhood was a regular small-town neighborhood. It had brick homes and split-level houses with mail boxes at the curb.

Kevin and his family moved to Maudlin when he was in sixth grade. Right away, Kevin became friends with a boy across the street. His name was Jamie Peters, but everyone called him Bug. Kevin was very skinny and Bug was chubby. They looked like quite a pair.

Kevin and Bug became good friends. They were almost like brothers, and they are still best friends today.

Shirley, Kevin's mom, drove a forklift at a factory. Later, she became a hairdresser and ran her own beauty salon. Kevin's father lived in a different city, so Kevin grew up with his mom, his two sisters and his stepfather. Kevin's family was very close and they all tried to support one another. "The best thing my mom did was teach me to be a young man. Respect yourself and respect other people," Kevin said.

Kevin loved basketball when he was a kid. But there wasn't a hoop at his house. If Kevin wanted to practice without going all the way to the playground, he went across the street to Bug's house.

Kevin's mom knew how much Kevin loved basketball. Even though they didn't have a lot of money, one time she gave Kevin a few extra dollars because he wanted to buy a pair of Air

Jordan sneakers. Kevin had mowed people's lawns and saved all his money, but he still didn't have enough to buy the shoes he wanted. Kevin's mom worked very hard so that Kevin could feel like a professional basketball player.

Because his mom was so busy, Kevin tried to stay out of her way. During the school year, he played basketball every afternoon. In the summer, he played all day. Kevin would wake up, shower, grab some breakfast or lunch, then head to Springfield Park a few blocks from his house. "On Sundays, I'd sprint home from church to go to the park," Kevin said. "Mom would get mad at me, 'cause she'd slice the meat loaf for family dinner. I'd take three slices, put them between bread, have a big glass of milk and then I'd go."

He would take his snack and run to the park to play ball. "All the kids would be there. People coming to the park to beat you. We called them 'legends,'" Kevin said.

Most people think that school basketball teams are the places where great players really learn to play well. But Kevin learned everything on the blacktop court at Springfield Park. He gained confidence playing there. He played against other kids and they all taught one another. He improved his shooting in shooting contests. Kevin never got bored with playing basketball.

Kevin's mom said, "The baby-sitter would call me at work and say, 'I can't find Kevin.' But I knew where I could find him. Always on the basketball court."

Kevin's friend Bug was much shorter than Kevin. But he would join the playground basketball games, too. "We played before school, after school, every day," Bug said. "It would be raining with a half foot of water on the court. During the winter, we played so much we were always sick with colds."

Kevin became a much better player. He always thought about his favorite NBA and college players and tried to do the things they did. Kevin loved Magic Johnson, Michael Jordan, Malik Sealy and Chris Webber. He would watch them on television and learn their moves. His basketball skills got much, much better.

The games at Springfield Park were always very tough. Kevin had to play against the best players in the neighborhood. There was one boy who Kevin called "Goldilocks." One time "Goldilocks" dunked on Kevin so hard that Kevin fell backward into a mud puddle.

There was also a guy named Bear who played at Springfield Park. Bear was an older kid who is one of Kevin's good friends today. Bear was bigger and heavier than Kevin. He loved to pick on Kevin by teasing him about his haircut, his basketball skills and his clothing. Bear would do anything to annoy Kevin. He liked to make Kevin play badly.

One day, though, a ball bounced off the rim and Kevin leaped up to get it. He slammed the ball down in a dunk. After that, no one at Springfield Park ever teased Kevin again. Not even Bear. Kevin was the new king of Springfield Park.

Chapter Three

Not everything about basketball can be learned at a playground. Kevin didn't learn all the rules of the game or how to be a complete player and a good teammate until high school.

Kevin loved playing ball in high school. Even though Kevin dunks all the time now, he thinks that he did his most spectacular dunk during his freshman season with the Mauldin Mavericks. That dunk was made in 1991. Kevin said, "I got so high when I caught an alley-oop, I came down and wrapped my legs over this kid's shoulder, like he was giving me a ride." That's quite a dunk!

In high school, Kevin was already 6-7. He was still working on his skills, but his height helped him a lot. He also had Bug as his number one fan. Bug would always go to Kevin's games and tell him to try harder. Bug was always by his buddy's side, helping him out. Kevin said, "Bug gave me all kinds of crazy confidence."

Kevin's high school coach was Duke Fisher. Duke had played basketball at the University of North Carolina, one of the best college basketball programs in the United States. He knew that Kevin needed a lot of practice, so he drilled him hard. "This kid can do great things with the basketball," Coach Fisher said about Kevin. "And he was the most unselfish good player I ever saw. He didn't care who scored. The only thing he hated was to lose."

Kevin didn't lose very often. In his junior year of high school, Mauldin won 22 games and only lost seven. Kevin averaged 27 points, 17 rebounds and seven blocked shots. But he was playing against teenagers from other small towns and schools. He wondered how he would do against the best players from the bigger cities.

He soon got his chance to find out. In his

senior year of high school, Kevin and his mom moved to Chicago. It was an exciting move to go from sleepy South Carolina to fast-paced Chicago. But it was very hard for Kevin to leave Bug and his other friends behind.

Kevin, his mom and his younger sister, Ashley, moved into a small apartment on Chicago's west side. They lived only one mile from the United Center, where Michael Jordan, Scottie Pippen and the rest of the Chicago Bulls won NBA championships. Kevin was living near his heroes.

Kevin's mom got an office job and Kevin began his senior year at a much bigger school. His new school, Farragut Academy, had a strict dress code and some tough kids from the big city. On Kevin's first day at school, one boy threw a hot dog at him and wanted to start a fight. But Kevin tried to be friends with everyone. It was hard for him to be in a new school.

Once the basketball season began, Kevin showed his classmates how good he was. They stopped giving him a hard time when they saw what a superstar he was on the court. Everyone knew right away how much he could help the team. Kevin soon had lots of new friends. Kevin said, "They went from not talking to me, to calling me 'Kevin,' then to 'KG' and then 'Hey, superstar!'"

When Kevin became a Farragut Admiral, the team had their most successful season in school history. They won 28 games and lost two. They even won the city championship! Kevin averaged 28 points each game that year. He was named the High School Player of the Year. He also was the best player in a national All-Star game for high school players. Lots of basketball scouts started to notice how good Kevin was.

Like many other kids his age, Kevin dreamed of going to college after high school. He really wanted to go to Michigan, Maryland, North Carolina or South Carolina. But Kevin's scores weren't high enough, so his dream of playing basketball at a famous university probably wouldn't come true.

But Kevin wouldn't give up. He took the college admissions test twice, but didn't get the score he needed. He decided to try one more time. The third time he took the test, Kevin finally got a score that was high enough. But by the time he got his score, he had already made a different choice.

Kevin decided to do something no high school basketball player had done in 20 years. He took a big chance. He decided to go right to the NBA.

This was the biggest adventure of Kevin's life.

Chapter Four

The Minnesota Timberwolves were one of the worst teams in the NBA. They became a team in 1989. They lost more games in their first six seasons than any other team in history. Timberwolves fans were unhappy. They wanted a star player. So the team took a big risk. They chose a teenager who had not played college basketball — Kevin Garnett.

The Timberwolves sent their coaches to Chicago to watch Kevin practice with his high school team. They wanted to see how good he really was. They were shocked to see his skills. It was clear Kevin would be a great player. Most players don't get as good as Kevin was then until age 24 or 25. Or maybe never.

Sure enough, on the night of the NBA Draft, Kevin was chosen fifth overall. His name was called after Joe Smith, Antonio McDyess, Jerry Stackhouse and Rasheed Wallace. Kevin was very excited and he knew he would do a good job for Minnesota.

But Kevin's success did not happen overnight. Kevin was young. He did not have experience against big NBA players. He was still very skinny in a sport that has lots of pushing and shoving. Kevin definitely needed a lot of practice. Tom Gugliotta, one of Kevin's first teammates in Minnesota, said, "I can't even imagine doing it. I didn't play my freshman year in college because I wasn't big enough or strong enough. Here he is, 19 years old, playing against 30-year-old men and holding his own."

Sometimes, basketball was the easy part. Games and practices only took up a few hours of Kevin's time. The rest of the day, Kevin had to learn about life away from home. Kevin's mom visited him a lot in Minnesota, but she couldn't move there with him. Luckily, Kevin's buddy Bug moved to Minnesota to be with him. Kevin and Bug were both on their own for the first time and it was hard getting used to taking care of themselves.

In his first season, Kevin lived

in an apartment in downtown Minneapolis. He always wore his Walkman walking around the city. In his free time, he loved to play

Kevin with Kevin McHale on Draft Day

Sega video games. But Kevin mostly only had time for basketball. He usually spent whatever time was left after practice with his buddies who visited from South Carolina. Kevin said, "The average 19-year-old is calling home for money, bringing his laundry home. I've been doing laundry and washing dishes all my life. But I'm still a kid. I like playing video games, going to the mall and meeting girls."

On the basketball court, Kevin faced new challenges every day. Many NBA players wanted to see if Kevin could keep up. In one of Kevin's first games, Milwaukee's Glenn Robinson scored some easy baskets against him. In a game against the Lakers, Cedric Ceballos dunked over him. Kevin was having a hard time getting used to playing with the big guys.

Kevin's teammates tested him, too. They wanted to see if he was good enough and tough enough to help them win. But they all liked Kevin and wanted him to do well. So they would pick on him, but only to make him a better player. Sam Mitchell, one of Kevin's teammates told him, "We aren't against you, man. This will make you stronger."

There was one night when Tom Gugliotta passed Kevin the ball at the end of the game. Kevin took the big shot and missed. Air ball! Kevin was very angry. He knew he had to get better. So he practiced very hard.

Before long, Kevin was making those shots. In a game against San Antonio, Kevin played so well against David Robinson that Robinson gave Kevin an encouraging whack on the rump. Kevin even played in the Schick Rookie Game at All-Star Weekend in February 1996! When the Timberwolves played in Chicago two weeks later, Kevin scored 20 points against the Chicago Bulls — the team with Michael Jordan, one of Kevin's heroes! That night, Michael said, "If he continues to grow, he'll be an All-Star in two years."

Kevin said, "Whenever I play guys like

Michael and Scottie P. and Dream [Hakeem Olajuwon], it's a dream. You come in, you meet guys that you admired all your life." Kevin had never imagined that he would be playing basketball against his heroes.

Soon, Kevin became a starter for the Timberwolves. He led their games with his scoring, rebounding and defense. He also brought energy to the team's arena, the Target Center. Kevin loved to wave his arms in the air to get the crowd excited.

He wore rubber bands on his wrists. If he made a mistake, he would snap them and force himself to "wake up." He even wrote the names of family and friends on his sneakers in black marker, in case they happened to be watching the game on TV.

Everything was starting to look good for Minnesota's new star.

Chapter Five

By the middle of Kevin's second season, he got to play in the 1997 All-Star Game in Cleveland. There were many famous players, such as Wilt Chamberlain, Bill Russell, George Mikan, Julius Erving, Magic Johnson, Larry Bird and others who attended the All-Star Weekend. The league was honoring the 50 Greatest Players in NBA History that weekend!

It was a thrilling time for Kevin. He had played the part of Wilt Chamberlain in an HBO movie that had been filmed the previous summer. Now he was shaking Wilt's hand.

After the All-Star Game, Kevin was able to take the game ball home as a souvenir. Charles Barkley, another NBA star, asked Kevin for his sneakers and his autograph. Kevin said, "Charles said that when he's 50 years old and in his rocking chair, he wanted something he could look at and remember we played together."

Kevin was making good memories with the Timberwolves, too. They won 40 games in his second season. They made the playoffs for the first time ever! The Timberwolves had added another young star, Stephon Marbury, to the team. They were

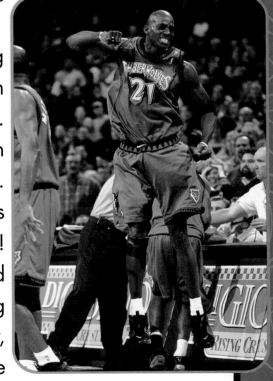

soon seen as one of the NBA's rising teams.

The Timberwolves did even better in 1997–98. They won 45 games and made the play-offs again. But the next year, Kevin's fourth in the NBA, Tom Gugliotta joined the Phoenix Suns and Stephon Marbury went to New Jersey. Kevin had to start all over again with a new group of teammates.

Minnesota made the playoffs that year and again in 1999–00. In 1999–00 they set a franchise record with 50 victories. But their playoffs ended quickly. Kevin wanted to do better. He wanted

After NBA great Wilt Chamberlain passed away in October 1999, Kevin played against the Phoenix Suns that night with Wilt's number "13" written in black marker on his ankle tape.

to win more than any-thing.

"Since day one, I wanted to be the best in what I do," Kevin said. "Not only as a player, but as a person."

Even though the Timberwolves didn't win any championships, Kevin made sure that he played hard and found ways to have fun. He made some funny TV commercials for

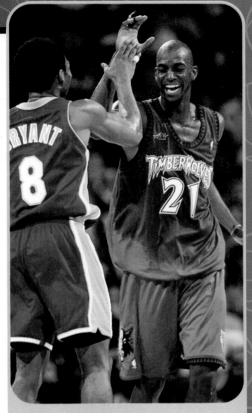
Kevin and Kobe Bryant

Nike. He starred as the captain of the "Fun Police" with NBA stars Gary Payton and Tim Hardaway. He lived in a big house outside Minneapolis and shared it with his dogs. Kevin had as many as 10 dogs at one time. He also had a lot of neat toys. He liked elec-tronics and gadgets, but he also liked his

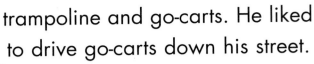

trampoline and go-carts. He liked to drive go-carts down his street.

Kevin found ways to have fun in life and on the basketball court. "I don't think you can put any kind of price on a player's love for the game," he said. "There are so many athletes like myself that would play this game even if there was no NBA, playing on blacktop, doing what they usually do on Sunday afternoons."

Chapter Six

By the end of the 2000–01 season, Kevin had already played in four NBA All-Star Games! He got to go to Sydney, Australia, to play in the 2000 Olympics. He helped the United States men's basketball team win the gold medal. Even though he was always traveling, Kevin continued to look out for his sisters and stayed in touch with his mom.

He even helped Bug and some of their other buddies start a business. They called it the "Official Block Family," or O.B.F. for short.

They dedicated it to the kids who grew up together on Basswood Drive in Maudlin, South Carolina. The business created a line of clothing, based on the type of things Kevin likes to wear: leather jackets, denim suits, comfortable sweatshirts

Kevin and his friends

and other casual clothes. Kevin loves to look good, but he's so tall that it's sometimes hard to find things that fit him. So he designed his own clothes!

Kevin loves music, especially hip-hop, rhythm and blues and jazz. He has recorded some tunes, but he hasn't produced any CDs as Shaquille O'Neal and some other players have done. One of Kevin's best friends in Minneapolis is Jimmy "Jam" Harris, a famous music producer. Jimmy is best known for working with Janet Jackson. Kevin has met Janet at some of Jimmy's parties.

In his free time, Kevin likes to play video games and watch TV. His favorite shows of all time are "Martin," "Good Times," "What's Happening?" and "Fat Albert." His favorite music is anything by Donnell Jones or Jay-Z.

After several years in the NBA, Kevin realizes how important education is. He has even taken some college correspondence courses! Even though he's busy leading the Timberwolves on the court, Kevin knows it's very important to find time to keep learning.

But Kevin's hardest job is trying to help the Timberwolves win an NBA championship. Last season was one of his toughest yet. More players were traded and Kevin had to get used to a new bunch of teammates. Minnesota won 47 games and made the playoffs again. But

once again, they lost to David Robinson, Tim Duncan and the rest of the San Antonio Spurs.

Kevin provided more leadership and energy than ever. "You always have to be the one to hold your head high, just so you can set an example for everyone else," he said. "But I hate to lose." Kevin will keep trying his hardest to help the Timberwolves win.

"I've always thought big and I always will," Kevin said. "You're never supposed to think small, because it's easy to reach something small. But if you have big expectations of yourself, that's special, especially if you reach it. I want the sky, and I'm not going to stop until I reach the top."